The Hunk-A-Doodles Find A Home

Eileen DiStasio-Clark

With Great Love and Appreciation to Those Who Have and Do Bless My Life.

My Family:

Joseph DeStasio Sr. & Miriam Lucille Baragone DeStasio, My Late Parents.

Andrea Jean DeStasio McIntosh, My Older Sister and Their Families.

Joseph DeStasio Jr., My Younger and Only Brother and Their Families.

Donna Marie DeStasio Wagner, My Younger Sister and Their Families.

My Children:

Eileen, Rebekah, Rachel, S. Michael,

Jennifer, Sharon, Tara, Stephanie,

Apryll, Mikaelah, & M. Trevor

and THEIR Families!!

ACKNOWLEDGMENTS

First and foremost, I express, deeply, my sincere gratitude to our Heavenly Father for blessing me with the gift and talent of writing! I know I could not do what I do without His assistance.

I also want to acknowledge and express gratitude to my children, Eileen, Rebekah, Rachel, S. Michael, Jennifer, Sharon, Tara, Stephanie, Apryll, Mikaelah, and M. Trevor, who were very active in 'creating' many tales about the Hunk-a-Doodles.

Truth be told, I really do not know how we came up with the name, Hunk-a-Doodles, but I give the credit for that to my children. I must also credit them for the inspirations that produced these stories because it was through their sweet and innocent childhood antics that they were originally originated!

INTRODUCTION

In 1992, shortly after my family moved to Missouri, I found, in a Clearance Sale Bin in the Hy-Vee grocery store, five stuffed fruits: a cherry, a lemon, an orange, a plum, and a watermelon. They were so cute I just had to buy them!

Once home, I put them on the half wall that separated the kitchen from the living room, where they sat for the whole time that we lived in that house. Now, of course, any time we had to move, they did too. We loved them too much to leave them behind!

In different homes, they usually sat in different places, on the wall above the stairs, on a bed, usually mine, on the back of the couch, on... well, just wherever we wanted them to sit. But sitting was not all that they did.

We played with them, we used them to decorate for special occasions, we... well, we just had a great deal of fun with them!

We called them our Hunk-a-Doodles, but I really do not recall how we came up with that name. We also gave each one of them their own name. The cherry was identified as Chad, the orange was named Ollie, the lemon was called Larry, the plum was Peter, and the watermelon was given the name Wally!

We also made up fun stories with them and that is what motivated me to write these stories to share with you! So, please read and enjoy them, over and over and over again!

THE HUNK-A-DOODLES FIND A HOME

Once upon an imagination,

In the Land of Never-Could-Happen,

There lived a bunch of Hunk-a-Doodles,

Who were always so busy mapping.

"Why?" you ask, "And what were they mapping?"

Well, that was something nobody knew,

Until the day Eniele and Lalpry,

A good deed, they decided to do.

Now, I think you may be wondering,

'Eniele and Lalpry? Who are they?'

Well, I will answer that question for you.

They were new friends who came by one day.

They wanted to help find a better place

Where the Hunk-a-Doodles could reside,

A place that was warm, cozy, and safe,

A comfy place for them to abide.

You see, they knew what most others did not,

What the Hunk-a-Doodles were mapping.

They had seen the Hunks in the valley,

While scary critters, they had been trapping.

They asked the Hunks, "What are you drawing?"

And the Hunks, this reply did give.

We are mapping the land all around,

So, we can search for a place to live.

Well, that was all it took! From that moment on, and I do mean that moment, Eniele and Lalpry also searched for a place where the Hunk-a-Doodles could live! And they all, that is Chad, Ollie, Larry, Peter, Wally, Eniele, and Lalpry, all searched everywhere, throughout the Land of Never-Could-Happen and the Valley of Down-Below, but found nothing.

Well, actually, they found a lot of things, a lot of different kinds of things, and saw a lot of beautiful things, but what they did not find was what they were looking for, a house that the Hunks could make their home. Until...

Hold on! Wait a minute! I have an idea! Instead of me just telling you their story, I think we should go with them, Eniele and Lalpry. So that you can see what they did for the Hunks.

Would you like to do that?

You would? Great! Then we will!! So, let us be going!

It was early one morning, as the sun was rising, when Lalpry heard a rap on her front door. "Whoa!" she said to herself, as she got up from her glider, "Who would be out this early in the morning?"

Then, no sooner had she opened the door; in fact, it was barely open at all when she heard Eniele, in a very excited, mildly commanding tone, say, "Come with me!"

"Where are we going?" Lalpry asked with curiosity.

"To Graceful Grove," Eniele replied, as she grabbed Lalpry's hand, pulled her out the door, and then closed the door with energetic force.

"Where is that?" Lalpry asked, sounding a bit confused.

"It is right in between the Land of Never-Could-Happen and the Valley of Down-Below! It is that place where, because there are so many trees, everyone thinks it is a forest. But I just learned that it really is not. On the other side of the trees, there is a grove,

5

Graceful Grove. And there is a house there that I think could possibly be the Hunk-a-Doodles' new home. It would be a great place for them to live!"

"I have never heard of that," Lalpry replied with excitement in her voice as she hepped her upstep. "How did you find it?"

"Well, I did not really find it," Eniele said, "I learned about it from my grandmother. You see, last night was our family game night, and while we were playing Shuck Your Corn, we were also talking, as we always do, about this, that, everything else, and nothing at all. And one of the things I mentioned was that we were trying to help the Hunk-a-Doodles find a place to live, but things did not seem to be going too well.

"Well, when I said that, all of a sudden, my grandmother jumped up from her chair, ran upstairs to her room, shuffled through a pile of… whatever she shuffled through, and then came back downstairs with a letter. She plopped herself down in her chair and then told us all to listen as she read the letter."

Eniele stopped for just a few moments to pull that letter out of her pocket. Then, as they continued to walk toward Graceful Grove, she read the letter to Lalpry.

My Dear Sweet Friend,

I hope you are doing well and I hope I can count on you for some help.

My mother has crossed the Bridge to Eternity and I am now left with her house and all her stuff. It is a very beautiful home and all of her things are in very good condition, but I do not need any of them because I have too much of my own stuff.

It is in the Graceful Grove, which we all know is so beautiful and peaceful, and I would not want anything for it. It would just be a gift from me, or my mother, to whomever would be sweet enough to accept it.

Do you know anyone who needs a home and would want my mother's? They can have all the stuff that is in it, if they want that too. Please let me know if you do.

Your friend,

Me.

Then, after folding up the letter and putting it back in her pocket, Eniele also said, "When she was done reading the letter, my grandmother looked directly at me and asked if I thought the Hunks would like to live in the Graceful Grove. She said she hoped that they would because she would really love for her friend's house to be gifted to them. So, before I take this letter and gift to the Hunks, I want us to go see it, not just the house, but the grove. My grandmother said it is so awesome!"

"Oh, my goodness," Lalpry exclaimed. "This is incredible!! Yes! Let us be going! I cannot wait to see it!"

Well, needless to say but I will say it anyway, so excited were they that both Eniele and Lalpry hopped, skipped, jumped, and ran down the street, through the parks and meadows, across the creek, and into what they had always thought was a forest, to the Graceful Grove, faster than they ever had, to anywhere, or for any reason. Once beyond the trees, they were stopped stone-still by their awe of the beauty before them. The sky was a crystal-clear blue, unlike any crystals or blues they had ever seen. The trees were magnificent beyond description! The meadows were placidly peaceful! And the house! It was the cutest little home either of them had ever seen!

After a few, well quite a few moments of silent admiration for what they saw, Lalpry said, "Eniele, I am more than one hundred percent certain that this is why neither we nor the Hunk-a-Doodles were able to find a place for them to live. We could not find a home for them anywhere else because this is the house that was meant to be theirs."

"Yes!" Eniele emphatically agreed. "I am certain that you are right! So, I think we should spend today and as many more days as we need to get it ready for them."

"Yes!" Lalpry said, "And I am ready to begin right now."

And begin right then was exactly what they did! They worked all that day and the next and the next. In fact, they worked everyday, except the Sabbath Day, for one whole week, moving everything out so they could clean the house and the stuff, sorting through everything so they would know what to keep and what to discard, getting everything ready in every way that they felt they needed to so do, and when they were done...

Eniele and Lalpry hopped, skipped, and jumped, trotted, loped and raced across the expanse of the Living Garden, all ten feet of it, to the Lofty White Wall, where they found Chad the Cherry, Ollie the Orange, Larry the Lemon, Peter the Plum, and Wally the Watermelon sitting, all of them with pens and paper in hands, doing what they always did, drawing maps.

***Side Note:** Because I think you may be thinking, 'What?! The Hunks are fruit? How could that be?' I am going to explain that to you. Even though the Hunks are not really fruits. Actually, nobody knows what they are that fruit, is what they look like.

Chad is round and red, like a cherry, and he has one lock of green hair on the top of his head that looks like a leaf and one lock that looks like a stem.

Ollie is round and orange, like an orange, and he has two locks of green hair on his head that look like leaves and one green lock that looks like a stem.

Larry is more oval in shape, and he is yellow, like a lemon, with one green lock or leaf of hair on his head and one green lock or stem with it.

Peter is round and purple, like a plum, and yes, he also has two green locks of hair on the top of his head, which looks like leaves, and one lock that looks like a stem.

Wally is round, and he is striped green and black like a watermelon, with one green lock of hair on the top of his head that looks like a big leaf and one lock that looks like a stem.

Okay, so now that you understand why everyone calls them Cherry, Orange, Lemon, Plum, and Watermelon, we will return to where we were before I brought us here.***

"Hi, guys!" Eniele and Lalpry called out, in unison, to the Hunk-a-Doodles as they approached the Lofty White Wall.

"Hello! How does it go?" called Chad the Cherry.

"Yo! We are so glad to see, so Howdy!" chimed Ollie the Orange.

"Hi, glad you came by!" Larry said.

"Hey, you made my day!" shouted Peter.

"Glad you blew in; how ya' doin!" Wally called out.

"We are doing pretty good," Lalpry responded energetically. "How are you doing?"

"Oh, I am fine on my line," Chad chimed back, "just sitting here mapping while I watch that maple tree sapping."

"I am okay; it is a good day," Ollie replied. "And I too am mapping, though I would rather be napping."

"I am feeling quite well, as you can probably tell," Larry said. "And I am also mapping, while I watch the birds' wings flapping."

"I am good, doing what I should," Peter responded. "And while I am mapping, I am also clapping."

"I am better than usual, feeling kind of musical," Wally stated with glee. "And, like the others, I am mapping, but I am also tapping."

"Well, good!" Eniele responded, "It is nice to know that you are all doing well. That is what we want you to be doing."

"Yes," Lalpry said, "it is nice to know that all of you are fine. And, while we do know why you are mapping, you told us why you now need to stop mapping?"

Seeing all of the Hunks hang their heads low, with sad expressions on their faces, and hearing them sigh, Eniele and Lalpry looked at each other, doing their best not to smile or chuckle and then asked, "Is something wrong? You all look so sad."

After a short moment, Larry quietly responded, "Well, we do not want to hurt you, and we know you know what we want to do!"

Then, Wally continued, "You have been kind and caring. Your efforts, with us, you have been sharing."

Chad took the next turn, and said, "And we definitely do not want to make any of you to feel sad or lonely or blue."

Next, Ollie added, "But we need to keep on mapping, or we will just be sitting here sapping."

Finally, Peter concluded with, "So, mapping we cannot stop, or all our hopes we will have to drop."

"Well," Eniele replied, "we know that you know that we know that you want a place to live. We know that you do not want to just sit on the wall all day and all night, every day and every night, and just watch over the Land of Never-Could-Happen, but that you want to live in the Land-of-Never-Could-Happen, or maybe in the Valley of Down-Below. In fact, we also know that you know that that is why we have been helping you search for a house."

Then Larry said, "Yes! A home is what we want to find, so as a family like yours, we can bind. We really do want to be with you, but sitting on the wall is a 'hard' thing to do."

After a moment of quiet chuckles over Larry's choice of words, Ollie continued, "And, though the Lofty White Wall is high, enough for us to feel close to Heaven."

Then Peter jumped in with, "It still does not feel like we are nigh to daily joy, not one of seven."

Now, because he felt that needed some explanation, Chad added, "The Lofty White Wall is beautiful, but it really is not a home."

And finally, Wally said, "It is hard and cold, high and... well, it is just not really a home."

Then, all together, the Hunks asked, "So, knowing that you know all that, why do you say we do not have to map?"

"Well!" Eniele replied, with great enthusiasm, "I will explain that to you. You see, we too want you to have a home. A safe and comfortable place to live. We do not want you to have to just sit on the wall every day and every night, in all kinds of weather. And, of course, we do not want you to end up going somewhere where you cannot be with us. That is why Lalpry and I chose to help you find a home?"

"Yes," Lalpry added, "and that is why we accepted your offer to use your maps to help you find a home so we could make sure that we covered all the land everywhere. But, what you may not know is that there is one place you did not have on your maps."

Well, needless to say but I will say it anyway, that really stunned the Hunks and they wanted to know what Eniele and Lalpry were talking about. So, they asked them what they meant and this, in the language of the Hunks, with Eniele beginning, is what Eniele and Lalpry shared with them:

"Every day, except the Sabbath Day,

We all arose with the sun.

Then each of us, in our own personal way,

After breakfast, began our search, which was fun!

"We wandered through the woods
And all the neighborhoods.
We roamed through the hills,
And ferried 'cross the rills.

"We searched the mountainside,
For places to abide.
"We combed the meadows and glens,
The valleys, towns, and fens.

"Day after day, from morning till night,
Against all the odds, we continued the fight.
Determined we were to find a home,
So, all the lands we continued to comb.

"But, day after day, no matter where we went,
We felt our time was not well spent,
Because, despite the fixedness of our minds,
Not one of us came back with possible finds.

"'We will not give up,' we all said,

Each night when it was time for bed.

We will continue to search around

'Til a home for the Hunks, is found."

"And search and search and search was exactly what we did, day after day, week after week, month after month but we found nothing. In fact, I remember when you all seemed to be so certain that we never were going to find anything. "

"Do you remember that day?" Lalpry asked. Then in Hunk-a-Doodle talk, she said:

"It was a quiet day, sometime in May, when Larry the Lemon was heard to say,

"A home, a home, we need a home; no more do we want to wander or roam."

"Down the street, he went to meet, his friend who really was quite sweet,
"Chad the Cherry, the merry cherry, who spent his days out on a ferry.

"But Chad the Cherry was not so merry when Larry met him on the ferry.

"A home, a home," said Chad the Cherry, no more do we want to float and roam.

"Up the hill, and past the mill, they walked, and walked, and walked until,
"Wally the Watermelon, they met on their way, but he was having a very bad day.

"We have no place where we can run, to sing and play and have some fun.
"A home, a home," said Wally the Watermelon, we are tired of always having to roam.

'Then off they went, the day they spent, looking for a house, or even a tent,
"When off the range, their direction did change, because they heard Ollie the Orange.

"He was up in a tree, too high to see, but they heard a sigh from a sad Ollie.
"A home! A home! Where is a home! It makes me cry to have to roam!"

"Back on the ground, Ollie found three of his friends waiting around.
"From out in the meadow, they heard a drum, and someone hum; it was Peter the Plum.

"Oh, hum drum," cried Peter the Plum, as his four
friends he saw come.
"We searched and searched, but nothing we found,
even though we searched all around."

Now, it was rather obvious from the expressions on
their faces that they did remember that day, which,
by the way, had only been about a week earlier. And
it also looked like they still had at least some of those
same concerns. So, without words, but after
communication with expressions, Eniele and Lalpry
continued, with Eniele beginning, and again in Hunk-
a-Doodle language, with this:

"Well then, Hunks, climb down off that wall, and
come and walk with us.
"And as you do, what I do not want you to do, is
make any kind of fuss."

As the Hunks did climb down off the wall, Lalpry
continued:

"Now come boys, and stay real close; we are going to
a place you know not.
"But we are certain that you will love, the gift for you
we got."

So, off they all went, on a trail that separated the Land of Never-Could-Happen from the Valley of Down Below, through the trees to the Graceful Grove. As they stepped out of the 'forest,' Lalpry and Eniele together said, with excitement and joy in their voices, "Here it is, Boys! Here is your home!!"

Now, as each of the Hunks also stepped out of the 'forest' and seeing the house that was in front of them, they began to cry, happy tears, joyful tears, thankful tears. In unison they cried out with inexpressible appreciation:

"Oh, my goodness, just up ahead,
There is a place to lay our tired heads.
A home! A home! There is a home!
Now none of us will have to roam."

"Wow!" they all said, "We see it now,"
And as they entered, they all cried, "WOW!"
It is not too big, nor too small.
It is just perfect for us all."

"So, on that day, sometime in May,
All five friends were heard to say,
"A home! A home! We have a home.
No more will any of us have to roam!"

And no more did they roam! For the first time ever, well, at least ever for them, they felt like they would finally be able to have a real life! Of course, having been on the Lofty White Wall all the time, they also thought they would need to obtain furniture and decorations and... well, you know what I mean; they thought they would have to somehow get all the things that they would need to make the house a home. But...

As they stepped up onto the porch, Eniele and Lalpry stepped in front of them, between the Hunks and the door. They asked them to sit down on the long porch swing that was hanging from the porch roof. Then, once they were all seated, Eniele pulled that letter from her friend, out of her pocket. Before reading it, she told them about the conversation she and Lalpry had had with her friend when they were having dinner together. She told them how curious they were when her friend suddenly got up and left the room, and how even more curious they were when she came back into the room with a letter in her hand.

While opening the letter, she said, "But when she read this to us, we knew that it was an answer to our prayers for you." Then she read the letter, and as she did, all the Hunks: Chad the Cherry, Ollie the Orange, Larry the Lemon, Peter the Plum, and Wally the Watermelon, all of them began to cry. They were certain that there was no way that they would ever be able to express the true and full gratitude and appreciation they felt! But their joy and their tears did not stop there.

Upon entering the house, they cried even more. For they did not see empty rooms and bare walls. Instead, they saw couches and chairs, tables and stools, beds and bookshelves, and… well, you get the idea, all the furnishings that they needed to make their new house a home. Now, while some of the furnishings were those that Eniele's friend's grandmother had left in the house, many of them had been given by their friends from the Valley of Down-Below.

From other friends in the Land of Never-Could-Happen, they also received pictures and paintings, figurines and knick-knacks, blankets and pillows, towels and washcloths, dishes and cookware... well, you get the idea. Everything they needed to be comfortable and cared for! And it was all in the house, waiting for the Hunks.

A trazillion tearful thank-yous were expressed by Chad, Ollie, Larry, Peter, and Wally. A gazillion hugs were shared with Eniele and Lalpry. And they were truly sincere expressions of the Hunks' real feelings.

Now, even though they did not have to furnish their home, they did have to take care of it, and that was something they had never had to do before. But, they learned quickly, with help from their friends from both the Land of Never-Could-Happen and the Valley of Down-Below. And once they were fully settled in their new home, they joyfully shared all the responsibilities of taking care of it.

They worked together to complete all the daily and weekly chores. They took turns sweeping, dusting, scrubbing, cooking, and organizing. They worked together in the yard, doing the mowing, raking, planting, weeding, and tending the fence. They gardened and harvested. They shopped and served. And, yes, everything they did, they did together. And, yes, they took very good care of their home. But they did much more than just take care of the house.

They lived in their home! They spent evenings together teaching each other things they learned from each other, from others, and from life! They had cookouts and bonfires. They took walks together, played games together, read stories to one and other, and so many other things.

But, most importantly, everything they did, they did together! You see, Chad, Ollie, Larry, Peter, and Wally were not just friends. They were not even just good friends. They were family ~ a real family!

They had learned from the L. D. S. that everyone really is a part of one family, God's family. So yes, they really were all brothers and sisters. So, that meant that Chad the Cherry, Ollie the Orange, Larry the Lemon, Peter the Plum, and Wally the Watermelon were more than just friends; they were brothers and that meant they were a real family. So, yes, they did everything together because that is what real families do!

But they did not stop there; they also invited their friends to join them, as often as they could, in all their activities And Rovert, LeChar, Eniele, Lalpry, Hakeber, Haleakim, Leachim, Einahpets, ReFinjen,

Rata, Norash, and others, all with their families, were always so delighted to share their time with the Hunk-a-Doodles. It made everyone so happy to see the close relationship between Chad, Ollie, Larry, Peter, and Walley.

And, as they worked together on all types of projects, played together in all kinds of fun ways, shared picnic time and holiday time, serious times and silly times... well, let me just say, as they gathered together for all kinds of times, it was very easy to see that they really were not just friends. Nope!! They were far more than friends! They were more than best friends! They were family, one big, happy family and there was nothing that any of them could ever have wanted or could ever want more than that!!

Now, so happy were the Hunk-a-Doodles to be able to, not just be a family, but to interact as a family that they promised themselves that every chance they got they would do all they could to share their family love with others. And they did, in some way, everyday!

Ergo, it was very accurately said that:

Chad the Cherry and Ollie the Orange,

Larry the Lemon, and Peter the Plum,

Wally the Watermelon, and all their friends,

Engaged as a Family—united as one!

Sweet as could be, soft-hearted and kind,
Working together all of the time.
They were more than friends, they were family!
And that was what they always wanted to be!!

So now, to you, they share this thought;
Since true family can never be bought,
Open your hearts and your love ever share
With family, friends, and all who care.

Then you too will know what it means
To follow the Father's Plan,
The plan that He designed
For all His children, every woman, every man.

Do well, that which He has directed,
"Love they neighbor as thyself,"
And true happiness will fill your life;
You will be blessed with Eternal Wealth!

The End,

Or is it

Another Step?

ABOUT THE AUTHOR

Eileen DiStasio-Clark is the second oldest of four children. She is the mother of eleven children and grandmother to twenty-three grandchildren, to date. As a member of The Church of Jesus Christ of Latter-Day Saints, she serves in various positions, teaching, leading, and ministering to children, youth, and adults. Currently, she is also a Family History Missionary. Eileen established the Pursuit of Excellence Institute of Family Education, a non-profit organization focused on strengthening the family. Presently she holds an A.A., a B.A., and an M.A. in Clinical Psychology and is working on the completion of her Doctoral Degree.

9 798330 546572